"Natasha Dennerstein's *Seahorse* escorts you as you 'limp your way' to the street and to the hospital room, collecting 'twenty-dollar bills,' 'gauze and sequins,' 'cabbies and truckers' in 'the afternoon Coors sunlight' toward the discovery that after all the 'blood-stained ribbon,' after all the fear 'of being clocked,' you, too, can 'do it / sooner, do it quicker, do it sooner,' you can, like the narrator, be a 'spy in the house of love,' 'survive / on sandwiches, apples, coffee, Marlboro Lights, / the kindness of queers' and arrive to where 'Now there is an "I."'"

- Matthew Clark Davison, Creative Writing Professor at SFSU and "The Lab"

"Natasha Dennerstein pops her poetry with culture, estrogen and brilliantly bold honesty. Reading this book brought me closer to myself, my sisters, and our shared histories. Trans is beautiful and Natasha illustrates how that beauty comes from hard-won victories over self and others. *Seahorse* is a well-cast spell. I'm so grateful for these words."

- Mx Justin Vivian Bond, Lambda Literary Award-winning *Tango, My Childhood Backwards and in High Heels* (2011)

# Seahorse

Natasha Dennerstein

Nomadic Press
2017

This book was made possible by a loving community of family and friends, old and new.

Requests for permission to make copies of any part of the work should be sent to info@nomadicpress.org.

For author questions or to book a reading at your school, bookstore, or alternative establishment, please send an email to info@nomadicpress.org.

Published by Nomadic Press, 2926 Foothill Boulevard, Oakland, California, 94601
www.nomadicpress.org

First Edition
First Printing

Printed in the United States

Library of Congress Cataloging-in-Publication Data

Dennerstein, Natasha, 1958 –
*Seahorse*/written by Natasha Dennerstein; illustrated by Arthur Johnstone
p. cm.
Summary: *Seahorse* follows the poet as she navigates the terrain between male and female. The reader follows on her harsh and rocky journey from the you of her youth to the "I" of her realized Self. Sometimes tragic, sometimes hilarious, this transpoetic personal odyssey can be appreciated by men, women and those intrepid souls who inhabit the places between. [1. POETRY / Subjects & Themes / Trans 2. POETRY / Subjects & Themes / Body. 3. POETRY / American / General.] I. Title.

2017937392

ISBN: 978-0-9981348-3-3

The illustrations in this book were created using pen and marker on Canson paper.
The type was set in Garamond Premier Pro.
Printed and bound in the United States
Typesetting and book design by J. K. Fowler
Edited by J. K. Fowler

*for*

*my myriad sisters and brothers*

*who died before their time*

# CONTENTS

"We delight in the beauty of the butterfly, but rarely admit the changes it has gone through to achieve that beauty."

- Maya Angelou

"And the day came when the risk to remain tight in a bud was more painful than the risk it took to blossom."

- Anais Nin, *The Diary of Anaïs Nin, Volume One*

# THE EYE OF YOUTH

"The eye of youth is very observant. Youth has its moments of keen intuition, even normal youth—but the intuition of those who stand mid-way between the sexes is so ruthless, so poignant, so deadly, as to be in the nature of an added scourge . . ."

- Radclyffe Hall, *The Well of Loneliness*

Hey, boy-child, you're expected
to be rowdy and rambunctious;
to bellow and demand;
to occasionally break the china.
Don't be so sensitive;
stop feeling so much for animals
and other people's pain;
stop crying. When you're upset and
you howl and howl like crazy,
you sound just a like a girl,
which is a really bad thing, boy.
You know there is something wrong
with you, you can see it in people's faces
when they cock their heads to one side—
like a curious dog—and give you that look.
There is something not quite right about you
—you have always known it—
everyone has always told you and
you sense that it is true:
you don't quite fit in.
You should kill yourself, boy—
is the thought that tintinnabulates
in your child brain—
you will never fit in;
you will always attract attention
and none of it good.
Oooh, boy—this isn't going to end well.

# HE WAS A SHE

"Holly came from Miami, F.L.A.
Hitch-hiked her way across the U.S.A.
Plucked her eyebrows on the way
Shaved her legs and then he was a she . . ."

- Lou Reed, "Walk On The Wild Side"

You watch 40s movies on daytime TV in black and white
and buy the same dresses for a dollar in thrift stores:
tight, flared, ruched; satin, silk, taffeta. Berets.

You tear your fishnet pantihose but keep wearing them, holey, to dances, bars,
parties with speed, booze, hashish, pills. You are fifteen and hitchhike. A lot.

You have furtive sex with cabbies and truckers: you learn
what you like and quickly learn how to get it. Sometimes
they give you money; then you start asking for it.

You stagger around in platform heels and hear in your mind
Lou Reed, David Bowie, Roxy Music. You try to look glamorous but hardly feel it.
You're a hot mess, girl.

The world is trying to destroy you; you learn to survive out of
spite. You won't let the bastards grind you down. You foam
pad your A-cups, straighten your seams, hope for the best.

# EITHER / OR

"You're more than just neither, honey. There's other ways to be than either-or. It's not so simple. Otherwise there wouldn't be so many people who don't fit."

- Leslie Feinberg, *Stone Butch Blues*

You just can't impersonate a straight man
or a gay one either. You just want to be a woman.
You dream of a life as female,

envisage yourself floating through trains
and offices in gauzy dresses,
other people treating you

like a special princess, instead
of recoiling from you,
gazing at you with scorn.

You hear of others who have changed gender, you
see a few drag queens and crossdressers
and wonder whether you might be

one of them, one of them. You
befriend showgirls and prostitutes,
take their black-market hormones

but can't get a regular supply. You
don't know if this is the right path for you,
yet can see no other options: there is no other path.

# ESTROGEN

"I was born twice: first, as a baby girl, on a remarkably smogless Detroit day in January of 1960; and then again, as a teenage boy, in an emergency room near Petoskey, Michigan, in August of 1974."

- Jeffrey Eugenides, *Middlesex*

**E** strogen—you feminizing chemical—she loves how you plump her up, making her flesh ripe and juicy like a young chicken, how you come from Woman and give Life, how you bring out her girly qualities, you.

**S** wallowed with a glass of water every morning, how she can feel you first in her nipples, itching with the pain of growth—bone pain in the hips—signifying change.

**T** hree blue pills.

**R** elease the feminine divine in her, estrogen, how you work your magic.

**O** istros: Greek for *verve* or *inspiration* and she loves how you give her that, estrogen.

**G** rowth of secondary sexual characteristics to prepare for child birth—tits and ass—adipose fatty tissue deposits and breast feeding. How you make a girl feel fecund, ripe.

**E** motional range and how you expand it, ethinyl estrodial.

**N** ever going back, never re-androgenizing. How you make her feel that femininity is the natural state for her and long may it last and how she loves you, estrogen.

## MUCH TOO FAST

"So I turned myself to face me
But I've never caught a glimpse
Of how the others must see the faker
I'm much too fast to take that test . . ."

- David Bowie, "Changes"

You feel self-conscious, dress androgynous—marle sweat pants,
yellow hoodie, kung-fu shoes—nothing incriminating you as trying

too hard to be male or female. You are embarrassed about your
facial hair, growing it out long enough to be zapped

with electric needles—regularly and painfully—like prolonged dentistry:
your punishment for daring to try to be a girl. You

keep wary eyes out for prolonged stares which are sometimes
*what is it's* and other times *va-va-vooms*. You are scared. Until one

day, you're walking on the street in jeans and a T-shirt, a guy you
knew before does a double take, eyes popping, jaw slack in

amazement and you know he's thinking *damn!* and you know it's working
and you know you're changing. And you like it. Suddenly

you've got hips, suddenly you've got tits, suddenly you've got booty and
suddenly you realize you've got a tiny bit of power.

You decide it's about time you got yourself a new name and decide to call
yourself *Natasha*. Why the fuck not? It's exotic.

# MISS WRONGBODY

"I was three or perhaps four years old whenI realized I had been born into the wrong body, and I should really be a girl. I remember the moment well, and it is the earliest memory of my life."

- Jan Morris, *Condundrum*

So you have your tits "done," and stay in hospital
overnight, welcoming the Elixir of Forget, relishing
the falling, falling of anesthesia. You wake up

feeling like you've been run down by a Mack truck,
with tight, sliced agony across your chest,
bandaged like an Egyptian mummy, but

you can't help smiling when you look down
and see a bulge where your bust should be.
Recovery is painful, especially running across the

street with those extra pounds in front: you
have to relearn your balance. You are delighted with
your new cleavage, figurehead of femininity. You

contemplate further surgery: nose, Adam's Apple,
vagina. You have no use for the appendage you were born with
and fantasize of a future where you're all Woman,

when you no longer have
your mother's features
and your father's fixtures.

# HARD BLACK EYES

"Lovely whore
with your hard black eyes
And your soft budding breasts . . ."

- Paul Verlaine, *To Dahlia*, translated by Walter Wykes

Electrolysis, wigs, pantyhose, hormones,
dresses, bracelets, earrings, hair combs—
it's expensive being a motherfucking woman:
dollars, baby, you gotta earn 'em.

No sooner than you count those twenties in
they go back out again: a never-ending parade
of folding stuff; you can't seem to get enough
dollars, baby, you gotta earn 'em.

Drug dealer, doctor's appointments, dentist,
nail artist, bikini waxer, hairbender, lawyer:
you can't seem to turn enough tricks for the
dollars, baby, you gotta earn 'em.

Your new tits prove to be an investment
so you jack them up front and center
and start to attract more clients with the
dollars, baby, you gotta earn 'em.

You have bulk sex and men give you
money. You guess you are a prostitute
but don't really care as long as you get those
dollars, baby, you gotta earn 'em.

# CAROUSEL HORSE

"she got herself a habit / she got it kinda bad
she didn't have the bread to keep it goin'
& she stood out on the street there; sold everything she had
& the cold winds from the south / they was a blowin'"
- David Mitchell, "The Ballad of Rosy Crochet"

You pull on your spandex minidress—light blue—
and jack up your titties in a push-up bra—hot pink—
stagger out the door in your scuffed-up heels—five inch—
to work the streets to earn enough cash
to buy enough dope to get high enough to work the streets.

You cop the insults, cat calls, potty-mouth taunts, cheap perverts
and just suck it up, girl. You gotta wear your thick skin
when you're out there, hour after hour, night after night
trying to work the streets to earn enough cash
to buy enough dope to get high enough to work the street, bitch.

You suck cock after cock and take plenty in the back door, carry
mouthwash and enema in your battered purse—leopard-print—
despite blistered feet and torn-up ass, you
persist in working the streets to earn enough cash
to get enough dope to get high enough to work the streets.

You count out your life in twenty-dollar bills, realize
that everything's got a price, even you. You get sick
to your stomach, sick to your soul but don't know how
to stop the carousel of working the street to earn enough cash
to buy enough dope to get high enough to work the street.

The occasional arrest a law-enforcement vacation
and a stint in detox or rehab a welcome break,
but you always have to get back on that goddam horse

when you work the streets to earn enough cash
to cop enough dope to get high enough to work the streets.

# WALK LIKE A WOMAN AND TALK LIKE A MAN

"Well, I'm not dumb but I can't understand
Why she walk like a woman and talk like a man
Oh my Lola.."

- The Kinks, "Lola"

Tits and a dick; stacked and hung;
she-male shenanigans;
the girl-with-that-little-something-extra:

this is how the world sees you, defined by
pornography. An in-betweeny creature;
a sexual unicorn;

a fetish object;
the way station for closet cases
that don't want to go the whole hog

and be a man with another man,
because that would make him "a faggot."
He can suck you off and feel okay about

himself because you look like a girl.
You hide your dick in the mirror
and dream of the day when it's gone.

# BONJOUR, MADEMOISELLE

"Then they gave me the final jab. As I murmured, 'One . . . two . . . three. Dr. Burou bent over and breathed, 'Au revoir, monsieur.' He smelt of gardens."

- Duncan Fallowell and April Ashley, *April Ashley's Odyssey*

You greyhound to Colorado, pass neat yards,
US flags waving in the afternoon Coors sunlight,
white-picket fence land, high schools, check in

to the mountaintop hospital. The doctor is kindly,
reassuring, explains the surgery. You sign forms,
get shaved down there, smell the orange antiseptic

paint, submit to the enemas, needles, crisp sheets,
brisk nuns, squeaky, waxed vinyl floors. A trip
to forget, time elapses, you wake up and look

out the window to a blanket of overnight snow.
The world has been carpeted clean, you feel
at peace, you are in a world of pain but you know

you feel right. You learn to walk again. When the tubes,
bandages are removed you see your self
in the mirror and say *this is me*. Now there is an "I."

I glide home with my head held high,
I am not *wrong* anymore; no longer
am I *wrong*; I am *wrong* no longer.

# SNOWED IN

"Look how white everything is, how quiet, how snowed-in.
I am learning peacefulness, lying by myself quietly
As the light lies on these white walls, this bed, these hands.
I am nobody; I have nothing to do with explosions.
I have given my name and my day-clothes up to the nurses
And my history to the anesthetist and my body to surgeons."

- Sylvia Plath, "Tulips"

I put on my lavender peignoir and admire
my self. Mister Mirror shows me my new vagina

and likes it 'till I pull the packing out—ribbon gauze
covered in gore—like the residual products of childbirth,

blooded, rotten: a Woman's lot. Stink, but I don't care.
Sore, weak, but happy. Friends visit, I make them

coffee. I insert the dilator, gingerly, tenderly, starting with
the small one, working up to the medium after seven

days. It's a procedure, but a bit erotic, if pain's your thing.
I feel like a young girl with a secret. I survive

on sandwiches, apples, coffee, Marlboro Lights,
the kindness of queers. I don't regret a thing. I heal.

# LOBSTER SUIT

"They're sexy
because they're needy,
which degrades them."

- Rae Armantrout, *Soft Money*

A background in the sex industry only prepared me for one thing: marriage. But when you're a tranny, straight guys wanna take you to the bedroom, not down the aisle. What could I do? I didn't care for people much: burnt out, hardened, wearing a carapace of emotional scar tissue around, like a bitter and twisted lobster suit. So I became a nurse—as you do—they care for people and get paid. I thought if I did the actions, the feelings might follow. And they did. Naked bodies, intimate cares of vulnerable people: it wasn't that different from prostitution. I found I cared. To a degree. Supplemented my meagre student nurse salary with a stint in the dungeon as a commercial Mistress: an occupation part acting, part cruelty, part striptease, part therapy and part nursing. I made enough to buy a small cottage, became a fully qualified Registered Nurse. They called me "Sister."

## POPCORN POPPER

"Either, deep in the dark of your history, someone showed you
that you could be used as a cash machine, as a popcorn popper,
as a rocket launch, as a coin-slot jackpot spunker, or they didn't
and you grew up unused and clueless."

- Jennifer Michael Hecht, *Gender Bender*

Fetishized, sexualized, aware of my self worth only in terms of who
wanted me, how attractive I was—or wasn't—I had to unlearn

a whole lot of stuff, learn some new stuff. Older women were my teachers,
my witches. I had to develop some interests and brand new skill sets,

had to learn when men were listening to me or looking me up and down,
had to befriend women—see them as allies, not competitors—had to

watch smart women and do like they did, comport myself like them.
I fully joined the female race as a card-carrying member, started

to learn how to earn the title, *Sister.* Had to learn, when introduced to
a couple, to focus on her, converse with her, give him politeness

but my attention to the woman. That's why I could only relax in queer
environments: I didn't know the arcane rules of heterosexuality.

Street cunning turned me into a quick learner. I moved
freely between many worlds: a spy in the house of love.

# MULTI-FACETED DIAMOND

"Now that I've solved my gender crisis, I've still got to come to grips with the other parts of life that go into making a happy individual: living a productive existence; having time for other human beings; having time for passion and compassion; having the time to create and shape the multi-faceted diamond that a fine life can be."

- Wendy Carlos, interview, *Playboy Magazine*

There is a place with a mauve pool
where the water is always warm
and effervescent. Lime willow fronds

shimmer apricot gold in the dappled
sunlight and all sounds are
muffled. Heroin used to take me there

but then you did, you did. We frolicked around
in our co-dependent mauve pool together,
like sea horses, tails locked, twirling around

an underwater plant. There were
other lovers before you, others after,
but I'm glad we had those years.

# FATHER TIME SURE GAVE HER A SPANKING

"Time doth transfix the flourish set on youth,
And delves the parallels in beauty's brow,
Feeds on the rarities of nature's truth,
And nothing stands but for his scythe to mow."

- Shakespeare, "Sonnet 60"

No template exists for an aging trans woman: we generally die before forty-five—by suicide, by neglect, by being strangled and locked in the trunk of a Buick Riviera and / or thrown into a river, by poor care, or by overdose when the thing we take to take away the pain eventually destroys us. I survived, learnt to take care of myself, got my teeth fixed, moisturized, mothered myself. The world judges my success by appearances yet the real meaningful growth has been internal, self acceptance, comfortability in my own skin. It took me fifty years, but I got here, I got here. Young people of all genders, I wish the same for you, but do it sooner, do it quicker, do it sooner.

# NON, JE NE REGRETTE RIEN

"If you are trying to transform a brutalized society into one where people can live in dignity and hope, you begin with the empowering of the most powerless. You build from the ground up."

- Adrienne Rich, "Going There and Being Here," *Blood, Bread and Poetry: Selected Prose*

There's nothing sadder than somebody who's had genital surgery
and regrets it because you can't unring a bell / the first cut is the deepest

and all that, but lucky for me I love being a woman—despite
a lifetime of treatment as a second-class citizen and being deemed not to be

authentic enough although feeling very authentic, as if there can be
degrees of authenticity—you know the French call us *femmes synthetique*,

plastic women and I don't mind because they say if you can't have children then
you're not really something something but who cares, it's the price

you pay and you can't have it all, but you can, you can.
Would I undo anything? Hell, no! I'm a transbitch and straddle the world of

gender and therefore have special knowledge, special powers: I can cross my
legs like a woman while folding my arms like a man.

# FEMALE PRONOUNS, PLEASE

"Frankly, I'm not responsible for other people's perceptions and what they consider real or fake. We must abolish the entitlement that deludes us into believing that we have the right to make assumptions about people's identities and project those assumptions onto their genders and bodies."

- Janet Mock, *Redefining Realness: My Path to Womanhood, Identity, Love & So Much More*

You limp your way to womanhood,
trying on images and stereotypes like
garments—shedding blood-stained ribbon

gauze and sequins—earning the hard way
the right to call yourselves woman,
utilizing synthesized hormones

(pregnant mare's urine)
to slough off your skins of acquired
masculinity to reveal the underlying

female, to shed, to shed to be the woman
within, to earn the title woman,
to be she, to be she, to be she.

# FEAR NOTHING, MISS THING

"Her life didn't revolve, but spun centrifugally, around stimulants, opiates, johns (who paid for her to dance for them in women's panties then ripped them off her . . ."

- *Last Exit to Brooklyn: A Novel*, Hugh Selby Jr.

As a child, all the time scared: scared of getting in trouble; scared of doing the wrong thing; scared of liking the wrong stuff; too fearful to give full throttle to my voice; fearful of being beaten up; ridiculed, always ridiculed.

As a young transgirl: scared on the streets; scared of being clocked; scared of officials; making myself smaller to evade detection, to avoid censure and violence.

As a woman, scared of somebody saying something, 'till I felt comfortable in my skin, then something happened and you know what? One day I just had enough of running scared. Enough stealth. "Passing" is a useless concept devised by the right wing.

Now not scared any more. Now refuse to make myself small; now speaking with my full voice. I will not be going back to fear. Once you're out of the closet, there's no going back: the closet has a one-way door.

# ACKNOWLEDGEMENTS

Many thanks to the editors of the following journals in which some of these poems will appear, sometimes in slightly different versions: "He Was a She" forthcoming in *Foglifter, Volume 2, Issue 1* (April 2017), "Miss Wrongbody" forthcoming in *Jam Tarts #4* (July 2017).

Thank you to my BATWW (Bay Area Trans Writers Workshop) colleagues for constructive and honest feedback on some of these pieces: y'all let me know this work was valuable, entertaining and worth pursuing. Thanks to J. K. Fowler, MK Chavez, and Cassandra Dallett of the Nomadic Press family: y'all drew me in by osmosis and let me know that my voice was relevant and necessary. *Seahorse* could not have happened with any other press.

**NATASHA DENNERSTEIN** was born in Melbourne, Australia, to a family originating in Belarus. She worked as a psychiatric nurse for many years, which gave her an interesting perspective on the human condition. She has an MFA from San Francisco State University. Natasha has had poetry published in many journals, including *Landfall*, *Snorkel*, *Shenandoah*, *Bloom*, *Transfer*, *Red Light Lit*, *Spoon River Poetry Review*, and *Foglifter*. Her collections *Anatomize* (2015) and *Triptych Californ* (2016) were published by Norfolk Press in San Francisco.